AAT

Final Accounts Preparation

Pocket Notes

These Pocket Notes support study for the following AAT qualifications:
AAT Advanced Diploma in Accounting – Level 3
AAT Advanced Certificate in Bookkeeping – Level 3
AAT Advanced Diploma in Accounting at SCQF Level 6

British library cataloguing-in-publication data

A catalogue record for this book is available from the British Library.

Published by:
Kaplan Publishing UK
Unit 2 The Business Centre
Molly Millars Lane
Wokingham
Berkshire
RG41 2QZ

ISBN 978-1-78740-544-8

© Kaplan Financial Limited, 2019

Printed and bound in Great Britain.

The text in this material and any others made available by any Kaplan Group company does not amount to advice on a particular matter and should not be taken as such. No reliance should be placed on the content as the basis for any investment or other decision or in connection with any advice given to third parties. Please consult your appropriate professional adviser as necessary. Kaplan Publishing Limited and all other Kaplan group companies expressly disclaim all liability to any person in respect of any losses or other claims, whether direct, indirect, incidental, consequential or otherwise arising in relation to the use of such materials.

All rights reserved. No part of this publication may be reproduced, stored in a retrieval system, or transmitted, in any form or by any means, electronic, mechanical, photocopying, recording or otherwise, without the prior written permission of Kaplan Publishing.

Final Accounts Preparation

Contents

		Study Text Chapter	Page Number
A guide to the assessment			1
Chapter 1	Sole trader accounts	1	5
Chapter 2	Partnership accounts	2	23
Chapter 3	Incomplete records	3	43
Chapter 4	Financial reporting and ethical principles	4	67
Index			I.1

Preface

These Pocket Notes contain the key points you need to know for the exam, presented in a unique visual way that makes revision easy and effective.

Written by experienced lecturers and authors, these Pocket Notes break down content into manageable chunks to maximise your concentration.

Quality and accuracy are of the utmost importance to us so if you spot an error in any of our products, please send an email to mykaplanreporting@kaplan.com with full details, or follow the link to the feedback form in MyKaplan.

Our Quality Co-ordinator will work with our technical team to verify the error and take action to ensure it is corrected in future editions

A guide to the assessment

A guide to the assessment

Overview of the assessment

The assessment

Final Accounts Preparation (FAPR) is the second of two financial accounting assessments at the Advanced Diploma level of the AAT qualification. We recommend that the Advanced Bookkeeping (AVBK) unit is studied and taken before FAPR.

Examination

FAPR is assessed by means of a computer based assessment (CBA). The CBA will last for 2 hours and will consist of 6 tasks.

In any one assessment, learners may not be assessed on all content, or on the full depth or breadth of a piece of content. The content assessed may change over time to ensure validity of assessment, but all assessment criteria will be assessed over time.

Learning outcomes & weighting

1. Distinguish between the financial recording and reporting requirements of different types of organisation — 10%

2. Explain the need for final accounts and the accounting and ethical principles underlying their preparation — 7%

3. Prepare accounting records from incomplete information — 27%

4. Produce accounts for sole traders — 31%

5. Produce accounts for partnerships — 20%

6. Recognise the key differences between preparing accounts for a limited company and a sole trader — 5%

Total — 100%

Pass mark

To pass a unit assessment, students need to achieve a mark of 70% or more

This unit contributes 15% of the total amount required for the Advanced Diploma in Accounting qualification.

Note on the Conceptual Framework

The Conceptual Framework for Financial Reporting 2010 identifies one assumption underlying the preparation of financial statements – the going concern assumption. However, the AAT have confirmed that the unit specification for Final Accounts Preparation departs from this and states that there are two underlying assumptions; going concern and the accruals basis.

chapter 1

Sole trader accounts

- Closing off ledger accounts.
- Drawings.
- Preparing final accounts from an extended trial balance.
- Preparing final accounts from an initial trial balance.

Closing off ledger accounts

```
Adjustments made in ETB
         ↓
Entered into ledger accounts
         ↓
Ledger accounts balanced
       ↙        ↘
```

Statement of profit or loss accounts
- balances cleared to statement of profit or loss (SPL)

Statement of financial position accounts
- closing balances become opening balances for the following period

Example

Year ending 31 December 20X5

Accumulated depreciation account

	£		£
		1 Jan X5 Balance b/d	4,000

The accumulated depreciation account has an opening balance as it is a statement of financial position account.

The depreciation charge account at 1 January 20X5 has no opening balance brought forward.

Depreciation charge for the year ended 31 December 20X5 is £1,000.

Solution

Enter the depreciation charge for the year in the ledger accounts:

Depreciation charge account

	£		£
31 Dec X5 Accum dep'n	1,000	31 Dec X5 SPL	1,000
	1,000		1,000

Accumulated depreciation account

	£		£
31 Dec X5 Balance c/d	5,000	1 Jan X5 Balance b/d	4,000
		31 Dec X5 Depreciation charge	1,000
	5,000		5,000
		1 Jan X6 Balance b/d	5,000

Accumulated account – SFP – balance b/d $5,000

Expense account – SPL – year's expense $1,000

Drawings

Double entry

- sole trader takes money out of his own business for living expenses = drawings.

Double entry:

Debit   Drawings

Credit   Cash

- sole trader take goods out of his own business = drawings.

Double entry:

Debit   Drawings

Credit   Purchases

Accounting treatment

- deduction from capital in the statement of financial position.

Statement of financial position extract

	£
Opening capital	X
Capital introduced in the year	X
Profit/(loss) for the year	X/(X)
Drawings	(X)
Closing capital	X

Preparing final accounts from an extended trial balance

- take final profit or loss column figures and put them into statement of profit or loss account format
- take final statement of financial position column figures and put them in statement of financial position order.

Example

Extended Trial Balance

Account name	Trial balance		Adjustments		Statement of profit or loss		Statement of financial position	
	DR	CR	DR	CR	DR	CR	DR	CR
	£	£	£	£	£	£	£	£
Sales		40,000				40,000		
Purchases	20,000				20,000			
Inventory at 1 Oct 20X6	2,000				2,000			
Non-current assets at cost	40,000						40,000	
Accumulated depreciation		18,000		6,000				24,000
Sales ledger control	4,400			400			4,000	
Bank	1,000						1,000	
Purchases ledger control		2,500						2,500
Drawings	10,000						10,000	
Capital		28,100						28,100
Rent	2,400			500	1,900			

Example

The ETB from the previous page is continued.

Account name	Trial balance		Adjustments		Statement of profit or loss		Statement of financial position	
	DR	CR	DR	CR	DR	CR	DR	CR
Wages	5,600				5,600			
Heat and light	3,200		300		3,500			
Depreciation charge			6,000		6,000			
Accruals				300				300
Prepayments			500				500	
Irrecoverable debts expense			400		400			
Allowance for doubtful debts adjustment			200		200			
Allowance for doubtful debts				200				200
Closing inventory - SFP			2,200				2,200	
Closing inventory - SPL				2,200		2,200		
Net profit					2,600			2,600
	88,600	88,600	9,600	9,600	42,200	42,200	57,700	57,700

Example

Statement of financial position as at 30 September 20X7

	£	£	£
Non-current assets	Cost	Depreciation	Carrying amount
Machinery	40,000	24,000	16,000
Current assets			
Inventory		2,200	
Receivables	4,000		
Less: allowance for doubtful debts	(200)		
		3,800	
Prepayments		500	
Bank		1,000	
		7,500	
Current liabilities			
Payables		2,500	
Accruals		300	
			(2,800)
Net current assets			4,700
Net assets			20,700
Financed by			
Capital			28,100
Profit for the year			2,600
Less: drawings			(10,000)
			20,700

Alternative presentation format for the statement of financial position:

Example

Statement of financial position as at 30 September 20X7

Non-current assets	Cost £	Depreciation £	Carrying amount £
Machinery	40,000	24,000	16,000
Current assets			
Inventory		2,200	
Receivables	4,000		
Less: allowance for doubtful debts	(200)		
		3,800	
Prepayments		500	
Bank		1,000	
			7,500
Total assets			23,500

Capital and liabilities:		£
Capital		28,100
Profit for the year		2,600
Less: drawings		(10,000)
		20,700
Current liabilities:		
Payables	2,500	
Accruals	300	
		2,800
Total capital and liabilities		23,500

Note that the two formats of the statement of financial position show exactly the same information. In the first format, liabilities have been deducted from assets to arrive at net assets which is equal to proprietor's capital

In the alternative format, non-current and current assets are totalled to show total assets. This is equal to proprietor's capital plus liabilities.

Example

Statement of profit or loss for the year ended 30 September 20X7

	£	£
Sales		40,000
Cost of goods sold:		
Opening inventory	2,000	
Purchases	20,000	
Closing inventory	(2,200)	
Cost of goods sold		(19,800)
Gross profit		20,200
Add: Sundry income		X
Less:		
Rent	1,900	
Wages	5,600	
Heat and light	3,500	
Depreciation charge	6,000	
Irrecoverable debt expense	400	
Allowance for doubtful debts adjustment	200	
Total expenses		(17,600)
Profit (loss) for the year		2,600

Sole trader accounts

Preparing final accounts from an initial trial balance

Step 1
Draft journal entries for any adjustments/errors.

Step 2
Adjust ledger accounts for journal entries.

Step 3
Carry down balances on adjusted ledger accounts.

Step 4
Draw up amended trial balance.

Step 5
Prepare statement of profit or loss and statement of financial position.

Example

The initial trial balance of a sole trader at 30 June 20X6:

	£	£
Sales		40,000
Purchases	20,000	
Inventory at 1 July 20X5	2,000	
Non-current assets at cost	40,000	
Accumulated depreciation at 1 July 20X5		18,000
Sales ledger control	4,400	
Bank	1,000	
Purchases ledger control		2,500
Drawings	10,000	

Capital		28,100
Rent	2,400	
Wages	5,600	
Heat and light	3,200	
	88,600	88,600

The following points are also noted:

(i) Depreciation at 15% straight line is to be charged for the year

(ii) There is an accrual for electricity of £300

(iii) There is a prepayment for rent of £500

(iv) An irrecoverable debt of £400 is to be written off

(v) An allowance for doubtful debts of 5% of remaining receivables needs to be set up

(vi) Closing inventory has been valued at £2,200.

Solution

Step 1

Draft journal entries for any adjustments/errors

(i) Depreciation at 15% straight line is to be charged for the year

Journal

Debit   Depreciation charge   £6,000

Credit   Accumulated depreciation   £6,000
£40,000 x 15% = £6,000

(ii) There is an accrual for electricity of £300

Journal

Debit   Electricity   £300

Credit   Accruals   £300

Sole trader accounts

(iii) There is a prepayment of rent of £500

Journal

Debit	Prepayments	£500
Credit	Rent	£500

(iv) Irrecoverable debt of £400 is to be written off

Journal

Debit	Irrecoverable debts expense	£400
Credit	SLCA	£400

(v) An allowance for doubtful debts of 5% of remaining receivables needs to be set up

Journal

Debit	Allowance for doubtful debt adjustment	£200
Credit	Allowance for doubtful debts	£200

(vi) Closing inventory has been valued at £2,200

Debit inventory account – SFP £2,2(00)
Credit inventory account – SPL £2,2(00)

Steps 2 and 3

Adjust ledger accounts for journal entries

Carry down balances on adjusted ledger accounts

Accumulated depreciation

	£		£
Balance c/d	24,000	Balance b/d	18,0(00)
		Depreciation charge	6,0(00)
	24,000		24,0(00)
		Balance b/d	24,0(00)

Depreciation charge			
	£		£
Accum dep'n	6,000		

Heat and light			
	£		£
Balance b/d	3,200	Balance c/d	3,500
Accrual	300		
	3,500		3,500
Balance b/d	3,500		

Accruals			
	£		£
		Heat & light	300

Rent			
	£		£
Balance b/d	2,400	Prepayment	500
		Balance c/d	1,900
	2,400		2,400
Balance b/d	1,900		

Prepayments			
	£		£
Rent	500		

Sales ledger control			
	£		£
Balance b/d	4,400	Irrecoverable debt expense	400
		Balance b/d	4,000
	4,400		4,400
Balance b/d	4,000		

Allowance for doubtful debts			
	£		£
Balance c/d	200	Allowance for doubtful debt adjustment	200
	200		200
		Balance b/d	200

Sole trader accounts

Irrecoverable debts expense

	£		£
SLCA	400		

Allowance for doubtful debt adjustment

	£		£
Allowance for doubtful debts	200		

Closing inventory – SPL

	£		£
		Closing inventory SFP	2,200

Closing inventory – SFP

	£		£
Closing inventory SPL	2,200		

Step 4

Draw up amended trial balance

	£	£
Sales		40,000
Purchases	20,000	
Inventory at 30 June 20X6	2,000	
Non-current assets at cost	40,000	
Accumulated depreciation at 30 June 20X6		24,000
Sales ledger control	4,000	
Bank	1,000	
Purchases ledger control		2,500
Drawings	10,000	
Capital		28,100
Rent	1,900	
Wages	5,600	
Heat and light	3,500	
Depreciation charge	6,000	

Accruals		300
Prepayments	500	
Irrecoverable debts expense	400	
Allowance for doubtful debts adjustment	200	
Allowance for doubtful debts		200
Closing inventory – SFP	2,200	
Closing inventory – SPL		2,200
	97,300	97,300

Step 5
Prepare statement of profit or loss for the year ended 30 June 20X6.

Statement of profit or loss for year ended 30 June 20X6

	£	£
Sales		40,000
Opening inventory	2,000	
Purchases	20,000	
	22,000	
Less: closing inventory	(2,200)	
Cost of goods sold		(19,800)
Gross profit		20,200

Sole trader accounts

Less: expenses			
Rent	1,900		
Wages	5,600		
Heat and light	3,500		
Depreciation charge	6,000		
Irrecoverable debts	400		
Allowance for doubtful debt adjustment	200	(17,600)	
Profit for year		2,600	

Statement of financial position as at 30 June 20X6

	Cost £	Dep'n £	CA £
Non-current assets	40,000	(24,000)	16,000
Current assets:			
Inventory		2,200	
Receivables	4,000		
Less: allowance for doubtful debts	(200)		
		3,800	
Prepayments		500	
Bank		1,000	
		7,500	
Current liabilities			
Payables	2,500		
Accruals	300	(2,800)	
Net current assets			4,7●
Net assets			20,7●
Financed by:			
Capital			28,1●
Profit for the year			2,6●
Less: drawings			(10,0●)
			20,7●

CBA focus

In the assessment you will be given an extended trial balance or trial balance and you will be expected to prepare the statement of profit or loss and statement of financial position.

Sole trader accounts

chapter 2

Partnership accounts

- Capital accounts.
- Current accounts.
- Appropriation account.
- Statement of financial position presentation.
- Preparing final accounts for a partnership.
- Partnership goodwill.
- Admission of a partner.
- Retirement of a partner.

Partnership accounts

Capital accounts

- one for each partner (generally columnar)
- only generally used when partners pay capital into the business.

Debit   Cash/bank

Credit   Capital account

Example

A and B have been in partnership for a number of years. A put £30,000 of capital into the business and B put in £20,000.

Capital accounts

	A £	B £		A £	B £
			Balance b/d	30,000	20,000

Current accounts

- one for each partner (generally column
- used for transactions between partnership and partners.

Current accounts

DEBIT	CREDIT
Drawings	Salaries to partner
Interest on drawings	Sales commission partners
	Interest on capital
	Profit share

- normally a small credit balance being amount partnership owes to partners

Example

On 1 January 20X5 A's current account had a balance of £1,000 and B's had a balance of £1,500.

Current accounts

	A £	B £		A £	
			Balance b/d	1,000	1,5

Appropriation account

- used to share out net profit to partners
- according to profit share agreement.

Example

During year ended 31 December 20X5 A and B's partnership made a net profit of £48,000.

Partnership agreement

- B to receive salary of £8,000 per annum
- both partners to receive interest on capital balances of 5%
- A and B both receive sales commission of £750
- profit to be split in the ratio of 2:1.

Solution

Appropriation account

	£
Net profit	48,000
Salary – B	(8,000)
Interest on capital	
– A (30,000 x 5%)	(1,500)
– B (20,000 x 5%)	(1,000)
Sales commission	
– A	(750)
– B	(750)
Residual profit	36,000
Share of residual profit	
– A (36,000 x 2/3)	24,000
– B (36,000 x 1/3)	12,000
	36,000

Partnership accounts

CBA focus

Salaries and sales commission for partners are an appropriation of profit not an expense in the statement of profit or loss.

Calculating interest on capital and interest on drawings will not be required in the assessment, but you will need to understand how to record these items.

- all profit share figures from appropriation account must then be posted to current accounts.

Current accounts

	A £	B £		A £	B £
			Balance b/d	1,000	1,500
			Salary		8,000
			Interest on capital	1,500	1,000
			Sales commission	750	750
			Profit share	24,000	12,000

Drawings

- partners take cash out of business
    - Debit   Current accounts
    - Credit Cash/bank

- partners take goods out of the busine[ss]
    - Debit   Current accounts
    - Credit Purchases

Example

During the year to 31 December 20X5, A took £25,000 of cash out of the business and B took £20,000 for living expenses.

Current accounts

	A £	B £		A £	B £
Drawings	25,000	20,000	Balance b/d	1,000	1,500
			Salary		8,000
			Interest on capital	1,500	1,000
			Sales commission	750	
			Profit share	24,000	12,000

Statement of financial position presentation

- capital accounts and current accounts balanced
- balances shown in bottom part of statement of financial position.

Example

Capital accounts

	A £	B £		A £	B £
			Balance b/d	30,000	20,000

Current accounts

	A £	B £		A £	B £
Drawings	25,000	20,000	Balance b/d	1,000	1,500
			Salary		8,000
			Interest on capital	1,500	1,000
Balance c/d	2,250	3,250	Sales commission	750	750
			Profit share	24,000	12,000
	27,250	23,250		27,250	23,250
			Balance b/d	2,250	3,250

Statement of financial position – extract

	£	£
Total net assets (bal fig)		55,500
Capital		
Capital account – A		30,000
Capital account – B		20,000
		50,000
Current account – A	2,250	
Current account – B	3,250	
		5,500
		55,500

CBA focus

Partnership accounts will appear in the FAPR examination. Therefore you must be able to deal with the basic accounting for a partnership.

Preparing final accounts for a partnership

Step 1
Prepare the statement of profit or loss – just the same as for a sole trader.

Step 2
Prepare appropriation account and enter profit share in current accounts.

Step 3
Enter drawings in current accounts and balance current accounts.

Step 4
Prepare statement of financial position – just the same as for a sole trader other than the capital section (see on previous page).

Example

C and D have been in partnership for a number of years sharing profits and losses equally and with interest on capital balances at 5% per annum.

Trial balance at 31 December 20X5:

	£	£
Sales		75,000
Purchases	32,000	
Inventory at 1 Jan 20X5	3,500	
Non-current assets at cost	60,000	
Accumulated depreciation at 1 Jan 20X5		26,000
Sales ledger control	7,300	
Allowance for doubtful debts		300
Bank	2,200	
Purchases ledger control		3,800

Drawings – C	12,000
Drawings – D	11,000
Capital account – C	20,000
Capital account – D	10,000
Current account – C	2,100
Current account – D	1,700
Rent	3,000
Advertising	3,800
Heat and light	4,100
	138,900 138,900

The following adjustments are to be made:

(i) Depreciation at 10% straight line is to be charged for the year

(ii) There is an accrual for advertising of £500

(iii) The allowance for doubtful debts is to be increased to £400

(iv) Closing inventory has been valued at £4,000.

Solution

Step 1

Prepare the statement of profit or loss – just the same as for a sole trader.

C and D Partnership

Statement of profit or loss for the year ended 31 December 20X5

	£	£
Sales		75,000
Opening inventory	3,500	
Purchases	32,000	
	35,500	
Less: closing inventory	(4,000)	
Cost of goods sold		31,500
Gross profit		43,500

Partnership accounts

	£	£
Less: expenses		
Rent	3,000	
Advertising (3,800 + 500)	4,300	
Heat and light	4,100	
Depreciation charge (60,000 x 10%)	6,000	
Allowance for doubtful debts adjustment (400 – 300)	100	
		(17,500)
Profit		26,000

Step 2

Prepare appropriation account and enter profit share in current accounts.

	£	£
Profit		26,00
Interest on capital –		
C (20,000 x 5%)		(1,00
D (10,000 x 5%)		(50
Residual profit		24,50
Profit share –		
C (24,500/2)		12,25
D (24,500/2)		12,25
		24,50

Current accounts

	C £	D £		C £
			Balance b/d	2,100 1,
			Interest	1,000
			Profit share	12,250 12,

Step 3

Enter drawings in current accounts and balance current accounts.

Current accounts

	C £	D £		C £	D £
Drawings	12,000	11,000	Balance b/d	2,100	1,700
			Interest	1,000	500
Balance c/d	3,350	3,450	Profit share	12,250	12,250
	15,350	14,450		15,350	14,450
			Balance b/d	3,350	3,450

Step 2

Prepare statement of financial position – just the same as for a sole trader other than the capital section.

Statement of financial position as at 31 December 20X5

	Cost £	Dep'n £	£
Non-current assets	60,000	32,000	28,000
Current assets:			
Inventory		4,000	
Receivables	7,300		
Less: allowance	(400)		
		6,900	
Bank		2,200	
Total assets		13,100	
Current liabilities			
Payables	3,800		
Accruals	500		
		(4,300)	
Net current assets			8,800
			36,800
Capital account – C	20,000		
Capital account – D	10,000	30,000	
Current account – C	3,350		
Current account – D	3,450	6,800	
		36,800	

Partnership goodwill

Goodwill becomes relevant in partnership accounts when there is either an admission or retirement of a partner as it is another asset of the partnership that must be included in the calculations.

Admission of a partner

Example

G and H have been in partnership for a number of years sharing profits equally. They both have capital account balances of £50,000. The goodwill of the partnership is estimated to be £20,000.

They are admitting J into the partnership and profits will then be shared between G, H and J in the ratio of 2 : 2 : 1.

J is investing £25,000 of capital into the partnership.

Solution

Step 1

Set up capital accounts with an additional column for the new partner. Enter old partners' capital account balances.

Partnership accounts

Capital

	G £	H £	J £		G £	H £	J £
				Balance b/d	50,000	50,000	

Step 2

Set up a temporary goodwill account (asset account) by:

- Debit   Goodwill
- Credit   Partners' capital accounts in the old profit share ratio (PSR).

Capital

	G £	H £	J £		G £	H £	J £
				Balance b/d	50,000	50,000	
				Goodwill	10,000	10,000	

Goodwill

		£		£
Capital accounts –	G	10,000		
	H	10,000		

Step 3
Bring in new partner's capital.

Capital

	G	H	J		G	H	J
	£	£	£		£	£	£
				Balance b/d	50,000	50,000	
				Goodwill	10,000	10,000	
				Bank			25,000

Step 4
Remove goodwill by:

    Debit   Partners' capital accounts in the new PSR

    Credit   Goodwill account

Capital

	G	H	J		G	H	J
	£	£	£		£	£	£
				Balance b/d	50,000	50,000	
Goodwill	8,000	8,000	4,000	Goodwill	10,000	10,000	
				Bank			25,000

Goodwill

		£			£
Capital accounts –	G	10,000	Capital accounts – G		8,000
	H	10,000	H		8,000
			J		4,000
		20,000			20,000

Step 5

Balance off the accounts.

Capital

	G	H	J		G	H	J
	£	£	£		£	£	£
Goodwill	8,000	8,000	4,000	Balance b/d	50,000	50,000	
Balance c/d	52,000	52,000	21,000	Goodwill	10,000	10,000	
	60,000	60,000	25,000	Bank			25,000
					60,000	60,000	25,000
				Balance b/d	52,000	52,000	21,000

Effectively J has purchased £2,000 of goodwill from each of G and H. Their capital balances have increased by £2,000 each and J's has decreased by £4,000.

Retirement of a partner

Calculate all that is due to the retiring partner
- capital a/c balance
- current a/c balance
- share of goodwill

Pay off the retiring partner leave money on loan to partnership/pay in cash/or both

Example

K, L and M were in partnership for many years sharing profits equally. On 31 December 20X5 K retired from the partnership. At that date the goodwill of the partnership was valued at £30,000.

It was agreed that £20,000 of what is owed to K would be paid in cash but the remainder would be on loan to the partnership. After K's retirement L and M were to share profits in the ratio of 2 : 1.

Capital and current account balances at 31 December 20X5:

		£
Capital	K	70,000
	L	50,000
	M	30,000

Partnership accounts

Current	K	5,000 (CR)
	L	2,000 (CR)
	M	1,000 (CR)

Solution

Step 1

Transfer retiring partner's current account balance to the capital account.

Capital

	K	L	M		K	L	M
	£	£	£		£	£	£
				Balance b/d	70,000	50,000	30,000
				Current a/c	5,000		

Current

	K	L	M		K	L	M
	£	£	£		£	£	£
Capital a/c	5,000			Balance b/d	5,000	2,000	1,000

Step 2

Set up a goodwill account temporarily:

- Debit   Goodwill
- Credit   Partners' capital accounts in old PSR

Capital

	K £	L £	M £		K £	L £	M £
				Balance b/d	70,000	50,000	30,000
				Current a/c	5,000		
				Goodwill	10,000	10,000	10,000

Goodwill

		£		£
Capital accounts	K	10,000		
	L	10,000		
	M	10,000		

Step 3

Pay off retiring partner and transfer any remainder to a loan account.

Capital

	K £	L £	M £		K £	L £	M £
Cash	20,000			Balance c/d	70,000	50,000	30,000
Loan a/c	65,000			Current a/c	5,000		
				Goodwill	10,000	10,000	10,000
	85,000				85,000		

Step 4

Remove goodwill account by:

    Debit   Partners' capital accounts in new PSR

    Credit   Goodwill account

Capital

	K £	L £	M £		K £	L £	M £
Cash	20,000			Balance c/d	70,000	50,000	30,000
Loan a/c	65,000			Current a/c	5,000		
Goodwill		20,000	10,000	Goodwill	10,000	10,000	10,000
	85,000				85,000		

Goodwill

		£			£
Capital accounts	K	10,000	Capital accounts L		20,000
	L	10,000		M	10,000
	M	10,000			
		30,000			30,000

Step 5

Balance remaining partners' capital accounts.

Capital

	K £	L £	M £		K £	L £	M £
Cash	20,000			Balance c/d	70,000	50,000	30,000
Loan	65,000			Current a/c	5,000		
Goodwill		20,000	10,000	Goodwill	10,000	10,000	10,000
Balance c/d		40,000	30,000				
	85,000	60,000	40,000		85,000	60,000	40,000
				Balance b/d		40,000	30,000

CBA focus

In the examination you will be asked to prepare both a statement of profit or loss and a statement of financial position from a trial balance. It is also likely that you will be asked to prepare an appropriation account, a current account or prepare capital accounts to deal with an admission or retirement of a partner.

chapter 3

Incomplete records

- Introduction.
- Net assets approach.
- Use of control accounts.
- Mark-ups and margins.
- Gross sales margin percentage.
- Assessing the reasonableness of figures.
- Bringing it all together.

Incomplete records

Introduction

A business that has incomplete records has failed to keep complete accounting information.

Therefore it is necessary to create a set of key workings as shown in this chapter to prepare the financial statements after establishing the missing figures.

You may need to use these key workings for any task within your assessment.

Net assets approach

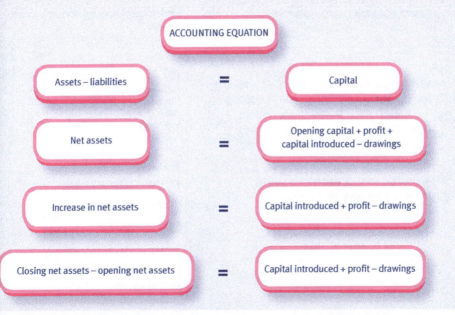

Incomplete records

Example

Assets and liabilities of a sole trader:

	1 Jan 20X5 £	31 Dec 20X5 £
Non-current assets (CA)	2,500	3,200
Receivables	1,000	1,600
Payables	(800)	(1,250)
Bank (DEBIT)	600	1,900
Inventory	2,000	2,700

No capital was introduced during the year but the owner took £4,000 in drawings. What was the profit for the year?

Solution

Find value of opening and closing net assets:

	1 Jan 20X5 £	31 D 20X £
Non-current assets (CA)	2,500	3,20
Receivables	1,000	1,60
Payables	(800)	(1,25
Bank (DEBIT)	600	1,90
Inventory	2,000	2,70
	5,300	8,15

Increase in net assets =

£8,150 - £5,300 = £2,850

Increase in net assets = Capital introduced + profit − drawing

£2,850 = £0 + profit - drawings

£2,850 + £4,000 = profit

£6,850 = profit

Use of control accounts

Cash/bank account

- used to find missing figures such as cash takings/cash drawings.

Example

- opening balance on bank account £2,000 positive balance
- opening cash float £200
- banked cash takings of £18,000
- paid expenses out of the bank account of £9,000
- paid cash expenses of £700
- closing bank balance £1,500
- closing cash float £200.

What was the amount of cash takings from customers?

What amount did the owner take out of the bank account as drawings?

Incomplete records

Solution

Step 1

Write up both cash and bank accounts from information given.

Step 2

Cash bank account

	Cash £	Bank £		Cash £	Bank £
Opening bal	200	2,000	Bankings	18,000	
Bankings		18,000	Expenses	700	9,000
			Closing bal	200	1,500

Look for the missing figures.

In the cash account there is a lot of money going out (bankings/expenses) but nothing coming in. The missing figure here is the amount of cash takings from customers.

In the bank account there is a large amount being banked but less being paid out as expenses. The difference is the amount the owner has taken out as drawings.

Step 3

Balance the accounts to find these missing figures.

Cash bank account

	Cash £	Bank £		Cash £	Ba
Opening bal	200	2,000	Bankings	18,000	
Bankings		18,000	Expenses	700	9,
Cash			Drawings		9,
takings	18,700		Closing bal	200	1
	18,900	20,000		18,900	20

Sales ledger control account

	£		£
Opening balance	X	Bank receipts	X
Sales	X	Discounts allowed	X
		Sales returns	X
		Irrecoverable debts written off	X
		Contra with PLCA	X
		Closing balance	X
	X		X

If three of the four figures are known, the fourth can be found as the balancing figure.

Example

- opening receivables £2,500
- closing receivables £3,400
- cash from sales £30,500

What are the sales for the period?

Solution

Sales ledger control account

	£		£
Opening balance	2,500	Cash from sales	30,500
Sales (bal fig)	**31,400**	Closing balance	3,400
	33,900		33,900

Incomplete records

Example

- opening receivables £12,600
- closing receivables £15,400
- sales £74,000

How much cash was received for sales during the period?

Solution 2

Sales ledger control account

	£		£
Opening balance	12,600	Cash from sales (bal fig)	71,200
Sales	74,000	Closing balance	15,400
	86,600		86,600

Purchases ledger control account

	£	
Bank payments	X	Opening balance
Purchase returns	X	Purchases
Discounts received	X	
Contra with SLCA	X	
Closing balance	X	
	X	

If three of the four figures are known, the fourth can be found as the balancing figure.

Example

- opening payables   £1,800
- closing payables   £2,200
- cash to suppliers   £19,400

What are the purchases for the period?

Solution

Purchases ledger control account

	£		£
Cash to suppliers	19,400	Opening balance	1,800
Closing balance	2,200	**Purchases (bal fig)**	**19,800**
	21,600		21,600

Example

- opening payables   £18,200
- closing payables   £16,100
- purchases   £88,200

How much cash was paid to suppliers during the period?

Solution

Purchase ledger control account

	£		£
Cash to suppliers (bal fig)	**90,300**	Opening balance	18,200
Closing balance	16,100	Purchases	88,200
	106,400		106,400

Incomplete records

Sales tax (VAT)

	£		£
		Opening balance	X
Sales returns day book	X	Sales day book	X
Purchase day book	X	Purchase returns day book	X
Cash purchases	X	Discounts received daybook	X
Bank - HMRC	X	Cash sales	X
Expenses	X		
Discounts allowed daybook	X		
Irrecoverable debts	X		
Closing balance	X		
	X̄		X̄

The opening balance on the sales tax account could also be a debit balance at the beginning of the period. This represents a balance owed from HMRC to the business. When balancing the sales tax account, either side of the ledger account could be the highest. This is due to the closing balance either being owed to or owed from HMRC at the end of the period.

Example

Given below is the summarised cash book for Joseph, a sole trader, for the year ended 31 March 20X7.

Cash book summary

	£		£
Cash from customers	63,425	Payments to suppliers	28,
		Payments for expenses	5,
		HMRC -VAT	3,
		Drawings	15,

All sales and purchases made during the year were on credit.

The owner can also provide you with details of the assets and liabilities at the start and at the end of the year as follows:

	1 April 20X6	31 March 20X7
	£	£
SLCA	10,500	11,200
PLCA	6,200	7,500
Sales tax	4,200 CR	?

(i) What is the sales revenue figure for the year?

(ii) What is the purchases figure for the year?

(iii) What is the closing balance on the sales tax (VAT) account? Round your VAT figures down to the nearest whole £.

Solution

(i) Complete the sales ledger control account to show the amount of sales revenue for the year.

Step 1
Write up the sales ledger control account from the information given.

Step 2
Balance the sales ledger control account by totalling the credit side of the account.

SLCA

Detail	£	Detail	£
Balance b/d	10,500	Cash received	63,425
Sales revenue (bal fig)	64,125	Balance c/d	11,200
	74,625		74,625

Step 3
The sales revenue for the year is the balancing figure on the debit side.

Incomplete records

(ii) Complete the purchases ledger control account to show the amount of purchases made during the year.

Step 1
Write up the purchases ledger control account from the information given.

Step 2
Balance the purchases ledger control account by totalling the debit side of the account.

PLCA

Detail	£	Detail	£
Cash payments	28,650	Balance b/d	6,200
Balance c/d	7,500	Purchases (bal fig)	29,950
	36,150		36,150

Step 3
The purchases for the year is the balancing figure on the credit side.

(iii) Complete the sales tax account to show the balance carried down at 31 March 20X7.

Step 1
Write up the sales tax account from the information given. Note: VAT on both sales and purchases will need to be calculated using the answers to parts (i) and (ii) of the example.

Step 2
Balance the sales tax account by totalling the credit side of the account.

Sales tax (VAT)

Detail	£	Detail	£
VAT on purchases (£29,950 / 6)	4,991	Balance b/d	4,
Bank – HMRC	3,500	VAT on sales (£64,125 / 6)	10
Balance c/d	6,396		
	14,887		14

Step 3
The closing balance on the sales tax account is the balancing figure on the debit side.

Mark-ups and margins

- cost structures provide a link between selling price and cost.

% added to cost to find selling price

gross profit as a % of selling price

Example

Find the cost structure for:
- mark-up of 20%
- margin of 20%

	Mark-up %		Margin %
Sales	120	Sales	100
Cost of goods sold	(100)	Cost of goods sold	(80)
Gross profit	20	Gross profit	20

Using cost structures

- if the cost structure is known together with either selling price or cost of goods sold, the other figure can be found.

Example

Mark-up

Goods with a selling price of £30,000 are sold at a mark-up of 25%. What was their cost?

Solution

Cost structure:

	%	£	Working
Sales	125	30,000	
Cost of goods sold	(100)	24,000	(30,000 x 100/125)
Gross profit	25		

Gross sales margin percentage

The gross sales profit margin percentage shows the percentage of profit retained from the selling price after deducting the cost of producing that good or service. This can be calculated as:

$$\frac{\text{Gross Profit}}{\text{Sales}} \times 100$$

CBA focus

In the examination, after calculating the cost of goods sold using either mark-up or margin, you may then be asked to calculate a component of cost of goods sold, for example, opening or closing inventory.

Example

Margin

A business sells goods at a margin of 25%. During the period sales were £50,000. What is the figure for cost of goods sold?

Solution

Cost structure:

	%	£	Working
Sales	100	50,000	
Cost of goods sold	(75)	37,500	50,000 x 75/100
Gross profit	25		

Incomplete records

Assessing the reasonableness of figures

Accountants should ensure that they are applying professional scepticism when assessing the reasonableness of figures provided in a given context.

Professional scepticism is an attitude that includes a questioning mind, being alert to conditions which may indicate possible misstatement due to error.

This should be taken into account when using the approaches to incomplete records, outlined in this chapter.

Bringing it all together

CBA focus

In the examination a typical incomplete records scenario is where you are given some asset/liability details together with a summarised bank account.

You are then asked to find sales, purchases and other expenses.

Example

John is a sole trader and prepares his accounts to 30 September 20X8. The summary of his bank account is as follows.

	£		£
Balance b/d 1 Oct 20X7	40,000	Postage	3,000
Receipts from receivables	80,000	General expenses	10,000
		Rent	10,000
		Payments to payables	30,000
		Drawings	12,000
		Balance at 30 Sept 20X8	55,000
	120,000		120,000

Receivables at 1 October 20X7 were £30,000 and at 30 September 20X8 were £40,000.

Payables at 1 October 20X7 were £20,000 and at 30 September 20X8 were £25,000.

Rent was paid at £2,000 per quarter. Rent had not been paid for the final quarter to 30 September 20X7 of the previous period.

During the year to 30 September 20X8 total payments of £3,000 for electricity were made which covered the period 1 September 20X7 to 30 November 20X8. You may assume that this cost was incurred evenly each month. Electricity is included in general expenses.

Incomplete records

Example

Task 1
Calculate the capital at 1 October 20X7

Task 2
Prepare the sales ledger control account for the year ended 30 September 20X8, showing credit sales as the balancing figure.

Task 3
Prepare the purchases ledger control account for the year ended 30 September 20X8, showing credit purchases as the balancing figure.

Task 4
Prepare the rent account for the year ended 30 September 20X8.

Task 5
Prepare the general expenses account for the year ended 30 September 20X8.

Task 6
Prepare a trial balance at 30 September 20X8

Solution

Task 1
Capital at 1 October 20X7

	£
Bank	40,000
Receivables	30,000
Payables	(20,000)
Rent accrued	(2,000)
Electricity accrued	(200)
Capital	47,800

Tutorial note. Remember that capital equals net assets. You therefore have to list all the assets and liabilities at the start of the year to find the net assets and therefore the capital.

Example

Task 2

Sales ledger control account

	£		£
Balance b/d 1 Oct 20X7	30,000	Cash from receivables	80,000
Credit sales (bal fig)	90,000	Bal c/d 30 Sept X8	40,000
	120,000		120,000

Task 3

Purchase ledger control account

	£		£
Payments to payables	30,000	Balance b/d 1 Oct 20X7	20,000
Balance c/d 30 Sept 20X8	25,000	Purchases (bal fig)	35,000
	55,000		55,000

Task 4

Rent account

	£		£
Bank	10,000	Balance b/d 1 Oct 20X7	2,000
		Expense for the year - SPL	8,000
	10,000		10,000

Incomplete records

Example

Task 5

General expenses account

	£		£
Bank	10,000	Balance b/d 1 Oct 20X7	200
		Expense for the year - SPL	9,400
		Prepayment c/d (2/15 x £3,000)	400
	10,000		10,000

Tutorial note. The £3,000 paid in the year for electricity to 30 September 20X8 covers 15 months. £200 is for the month of September 20X7 (an accrual) and £400 is for the two months October and November 20X8 (a prepayment).

Example

Task 6
Trial balance as at 30 September 20X8

	£	£
Capital at 1 October 20X7		47,8
Bank	55,000	
Sales		90,0
Sales ledger control a/c	40,000	
Purchases	35,000	
Purchases ledger control a/c		25,0
Prepayment – general expenses	400	
Rent	8,000	
General expenses	9,400	
Postage	3,000	
Drawings	12,000	
	162,800	162,8

Example

Given below is the summarised bank account of a sole trader for the year ended 31 December 20X5.

Bank account

	£		£
Opening balance	1,300	Payables	25,400
Receivables	41,500	Expenses	4,700
		Drawings	10,000
		Closing balance	2,700
	42,800		42,800

Other assets and liabilities were as follows:

	1 Jan 20X5	31 Dec 20X5
	£	£
Non-current assets at cost	10,000	10,000
Accumulated depreciation	4,000	not yet available
Receivables	2,000	3,800
Payables	1,600	2,200
Inventory	1,000	1,500
Accruals for expenses	500	600
Capital	8,200	not yet available

Depreciation is charged at 10% on the straight line basis.

Task

Produce the trial balance at 31 December 20X5.

Incomplete records

Solution

Find sales for the year.

Sales ledger control account

	£		£
Opening balance	2,000	Cash from	
Sales (bal fig)	43,300	customers (Bank)	41,500
		Closing balance	3,800
	45,300		45,300

Find purchases for the year.

Purchase ledger control account

	£		£
Cash to		Opening balance	1,600
suppliers (Bank)	25,400	Purchases	26,000
Closing balance	2,200	(bal fig)	
	27,600		27,600

Calculate the expenses for the year.

Expenses

	£		£
Cash paid (Bank)	4,700	Opening accrual	5
Closing accrual	600	Expenses	
		(bal fig)	4,8
	5,300		5,3

Calculate the depreciation charge for the year.

Depreciation = £10,000 × 10%
 = £1,000

Calculate the updated accumulated depreciation at the year-end.

Accumulated depreciation = £4,000 + £1,000
 = £5,000

Prepare the sole trader's trial balance at 31 December 20X5.

	DR £	CR £
Non-current assets (from assets/liabilities list)	10,000	
Accumulated depreciation (calculation)		5,000
Depreciation charge (calculation)	1,000	
Sales (calculation)		43,300
Purchases (calculation)	26,000	
Bank (from bank account)	2,700	
Drawings (from bank account)	10,000	
Receivables (from SLCA)	3,800	
Payables (from total PLCA)		2,200
Accruals (from assets/liabilities list)		600
Expenses (calculation)	4,800	
Inventory (opening inventory)	1,000	
Closing inventory – SFP	1,500	
Closing inventory – SPL		1,500
Capital (opening capital)		8,200
	60,800	60,800

Incomplete records

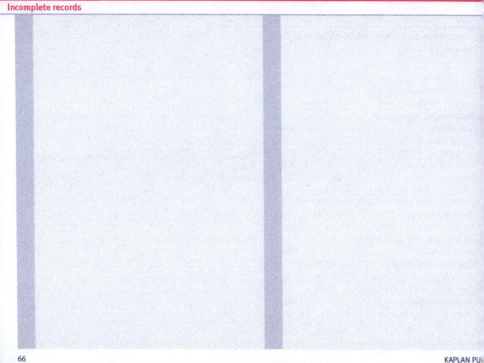

Financial reporting and ethical principles

- Introduction.
- Different types of organisation.
- Differences between preparing accounts for a sole trader and a limited company.
- Users of final accounts.
- The regulatory framework.
- The underlying assumptions.
- The fundamental qualitative characteristics.
- Ethical principles relating to the preparation of final accounts.

Financial reporting and ethical principles

Introduction

Different businesses prepare accounts in different ways as they need to comply with the relevant legislation and accounting standards.

There are also several ethical principles that need to be taken into account when preparing final accounts.

You will be asked about the reporting regulations and ethical principles in the FAPR assessment.

Different types of organisation

For profit organisations are businesses whose primary goal is making money (a profit).

Not-for-profit organisations are non-profit making. They are usually charities or other types of public service organisation. Charities must satisfy the definition of a charity found in the Charities Act.

Sole traders are businesses which are owned and ran by one individual. The owner is responsible for any business debts.

Partnerships are businesses which are owned and ran by two or more persons. The partners are responsible for any business debts.

Limited companies are classed as their own legal entity where the shareholders (investors) are the owners.

Limited liability partnerships (LLPs) are partnerships where some or all of the partners have limited liabilities similar to shareholders in a company.

Charities are organisations which meet the definition of a charity set out in the Charities Act 2011. It must be established for charitable purposes only, meaning that it must be for the general benefit of the public. It needs to be established for specific purposes for example the advancement of education, the advancement of religion and the advancement of arts and culture.

Differences between preparing accounts for a sole trader and a limited company

Legal requirements

There is no legal requirement for sole traders and partnerships to prepare accounts but they may find it useful to assess the financial performance and position of their business. Limited companies have a legal requirement to prepare final accounts annually in line with the relevant accounting standards. If the company has adopted IFRSs then it must prepare accounts in the format outlined by International Accounting Standard 1 (IAS 1).

Tax

Sole traders and partners in a partnership pay income tax on their share of the taxable profits. Companies pay corporation tax on their taxable profits and this will be charged to the statement of profit or loss as an expense.

Borrowings

Sole traders and partners in a partnership are free to borrow from the business bank account how they wish, this is classed as drawings. If the business bank account runs to an overdraft then the owners are personally liable for the debts. Directors (only) in a company can sometimes withdraw cash from the company provided it is within the limits set out in Companies Act 2006.

Users of final accounts

Investors (Shareholders) use final accounts to make decisions about buying, selling or holding equity in the company.

Lenders use final accounts to decide whether to provide loans or other forms of credit.

Other payables use final accounts to decide whether to supply goods on credit and the terms of the credit.

Management use final accounts to compare the performance of the organisation with that of other organisations in the same business sector.

The regulatory framework

All UK companies may use **International Financial Reporting Standards (IFRSs)** when preparing their financial statements. It is mandatory for listed UK companies to use IFRS.

Accounting standards give guidance in specific areas of accounting.

IFRSs are issued by the **International Accounting Standards Board (IASB)**.

The **IFRS Interpretations committee (IFRS IC)** assist the IASB in establishing and improving standards of financial accounting and reporting.

The **IFRS Advisory Council (IFRS AC)** provides a forum for organisations and individuals to input into the standard setting process.

Outlined below are three accounting standards which AAT may test as part of the Final Accounts Preparation unit:

IAS 1 Presentation of the Financial Statements

This accounting standard sets out the overall requirements for financial statements for organisations adopting IFRSs, including how they should be structured, the minimum requirements for their content and overriding concepts such as going concern, the accruals basis of accounting and the format and classification of financial statements. The standard requires a complete set of financial statements to comprise a statement of financial position, a statement of profit or loss and other comprehensive income, a statement of changes in equity and a statement of cash flows.

IAS 2 Inventories

This accounting standard contains the requirements on how to account for most types of inventory. The standard requires inventories to be measured at the lower of cost and net realisable value (NRV).

IAS 16 Property, Plant and Equipment

This accounting standard outlines the accounting treatment for most types of property, plant and equipment. Property, plant and equipment is measured at its cost and depreciated so that its depreciable amount is allocated over its useful economic life.

The underlying assumption

Going concern basis assumes that the business will continue in operational existence for the foreseeable future without the need or intention to cease trading.

Accruals basis ensures that transactions are reflected in the financial statements for the period in which they occur. This means that the amount of income should be recognised as it is earned and expenses when they are incurred.

The fundamental qualitative characteristics

The framework identifies two fundamental qualitative characteristics of useful financial information. Preparers of the financial information should attempt to maximise these characteristics to benefit the users of the accounts.

Relevance ensures that the information is capable of influencing the decision-making of the users of the financial information.

Faithful representation ensures that the information is complete, neutral and free from error.

There are also four supporting qualitative characteristics:

Comparability – it should be possible to compare an entity over time and with similar information about other entities.

Verifiability – if information can be verified (e.g. through an audit) this provides assurance to the users that it is both credible and reliable.

Timeliness – information should be provided to users within a timescale suitable for their decision making purposes.

Understandability – information should be understandable to those that might want to review and use it. This can be facilitated through appropriate classification, characterisation and presentation of information.

Ethical principles relating to the preparation of final accounts

When preparing accounts a person should always comply with the fundamental code of ethics.

Professional competence and due care

A professional accountant has a continuing duty to maintain professional knowledge and skill at the level required to ensure that a client or employer receives competent professional service based on current developments in practice, legislation and techniques.

Objectivity

A professional accountant should not allow bias, conflict of interest or undue influence of others to override professional or business judgments.

Confidentiality

A professional accountant should respect the confidentiality of information acquired as a result of professional and business relationships and should not disclose any such information to third parties without proper and specific authority unless there is a legal or professional right or duty to disclose.

Integrity

A person should be straightforward and honest in performing professional work and in all business relationships.

Professional behaviour

A person should not act in any way that is unprofessional or does not comply with relevant laws and regulations.

Index

Index

A
Admission of a partner 33
Appropriation account 25

C
Capital accounts 24
Charities 69
Current accounts 24

D
Drawings 8, 24, 26

E
Ethical principles 74
Extended trial balance 9

G
Goodwill 32

I
IAS 1 Presentation of the Financial Statements 71
IAS 2 Inventories 72
IAS 16 Property, Plant and Equipment 72
Incomplete records 43

L
Ledger accounts 6
Limited liability partnerships (LLPs) 69

M
Margins 56
Mark-ups 56

N
Net assets approach 45
Not-for-profit organisations 68

P
Partnership accounts 23

Index

R
Retirement of a partner 37

S
Sole trader accounts 5
Statement of financial position 6, 27
Statement of profit or loss 6

T
The regulatory framework 71
Trial balance 14

U
Use of control accounts 47
Users of final accounts 70

Index